As someone who has built their career around empowering girls and young women, I found Sylvia's book to be inspiring for anyone coming into their own and discovering their best self. Through her own personal life experiences, which she so humbly offers us insight to throughout these pages, readers will be able to not only find themselves drawn towards discovering their lives' purpose, but will discover that they are THE purpose.

—Breanne Ewing,
National American Miss
Missouri and Kansas State Director

Mrs. Anita!
The Diva!!!
... I Love You!!
Sylvia

Be you·ti·ful

Navigating through the Transitions of Life to Find the Real You

SYLVIA MARIE WATKINS

Be-You-ti-ful: Navigating Through the Transitions of Life to Find the Real You

Trilogy Christian Publishers
A Wholly Owned Subsidary of Trinity Broadcasting Network
2442 Michelle Drive Tustin, CA 92780

For information about special discounts for bulk purchases, please contact Trilogy Christian Publishing. Rights Department, 2442 Michelle Drive, Tustin, CA 92780.

Trilogy Christian Publishing/TBN and colophon are trademarks of Trinity Broadcasting Network.

Trilogy Disclaimer: The views and content expressed in this book are those of the author and may not necessarily reflect the views and doctrine of Trilogy Christian Publishing or the Trinity Broadcasting Network.

Manufactured in the United States of America
10 9 8 7 6 5 4 3 2 1
Library of Congress Cataloging-in-Publication Data is available.

ISBN: 978-1-63769-124-3
E-ISBN: 978-1-63769-125-0

Dedication

To my father,
Willie Ray Watkins,
*who taught me to
have a heart for people.*

To my mother,
Professor Anita Watkins Stevens,
*who taught me
how to work
and how to win.*

To my brother,
Minister Christopher Watkins,
*who taught me
how to have a servant's heart.*

Acknowledgments

To the author and sustainer of my destiny, my Lord and Savior Jesus Christ. You are the creator of all things and the lover of my soul.

Bishop Wilfret Lee…it all started with you when I was fifteen years old. You saw and continue to see what I need to see in order for me to become.

For at least a year, my childhood best friend, Philana Blakely, would send me text messages that included opportunities to submit writing samples to magazines and online companies. I would look at them but never really considered submitting anything. Little did I know that the deposits she put in my spirit with all those text messages would be the courage I needed to introduce this book to the world. I love you, Philana!

You may get tired of my acknowledging what you have brought to my life. My spiritual "mama," Marilyn Rhine Jones, walked me through some of the most difficult seasons of my life. My spirit would not have been healed in order to finish this book. You anchored me to continue to walk out my journey. Your "holy ghost" pushes me out of my comfort zone every time. I love you!

She went from labor to reward some years ago, but she taught me more about life than she ever knew. To Erma Gates, you fought a good fight, you finished your course, and your daughter Heather is definitely my sister for life!

To Felicia Keener, you introduced to me the *Be You-ti-ful* title because your heart was so open to my unknown journey at the time during that summer of 2015. I told you I would never forget, and I never will.

To Bishop Henry, Pastor Patricia Phillips, and the Power of Change Christian Center. Because of you, I came to accept that there was more for me. Once I learned to use my spiritual gifts and talents for myself, it changed everything. My years with you are seasons I will never forget, and the lessons I learned will last a lifetime.

To Lead Pastor Greg Holder, Pastor Rob, Pastor Josh, Pastor Patti, Pastor Lori, and The Crossing Church: for six years, you were there every week when I needed a peaceful place to land without judgment. From the Vision Dinner to being baptized again at the age of forty-three, the authenticity of the atmosphere you create gave me the clarity I needed to start this next chapter, and for that I will forever be grateful.

To my life-long sister/friends/family Shamika, Toni & Craig, Rachelle, Nicko, Nina, The DIVAS (Mrs. Williams, Mrs. Anita, & Nurse Mitchell), you all add more to my life than you know.

To my Grandmother Jennie Stevenson, who went home to be with the Lord years ago, who was the epitome of a writer; the Stevenson and Watkins family, I love you!

To the staff at Trilogy, thank you for believing in me as a first-time published author. This journey has added another chapter to my life story and gave me another opportunity to reach the world for God's glory.

Table of Contents

Be you-ti-ful:

learning the life lessons you need to learn
in order to be true to who you are
and what you have been assigned or commissioned
to do or become

Introduction

I remember going to Denny's with my sister Toni and her twins, CJ and Cortney. They were maybe six or seven at the time. Eating my favorite chocolate chip pancakes, I was talking to Toni about a few things I wanted to do, but I was uncertain about the timing. We ate and talked. As we were leaving and kept talking on the parking lot, the twins were jumping around like they normally did, and out of nowhere, Cortney said, "Sylvia, take a risk." We laughed so hard! Cortney has always been wise beyond her years. As I drove home, I clearly recognized that God had just spoken through a seven-year-old. The question was, *what was I going to do next?*

When it comes to career and business, I have never had a problem taking risks. I could take nothing and turn it into something. I knew how to plan every inch of an event. I could type out pages and pages of a script and then spend days editing what I had already written. I was the master of my game! The only problem was I didn't know how to transfer that same knowledge, skill, and attention to detail into my personal life. I wasn't motivated to try. I just didn't want to do it. Well, through a series of life-altering experiences and come-to-Jesus moments, I survived it all to share with you how I made it.

If you are reading this book, I am convinced that it's not an accident. I prayed and asked God to place this book in the hands of those who have experienced life-altering situations, come-to-Jesus moments, and they need to know where they should go from here. This book is a series of life experiences, situations, circumstances, and the life lessons I learned along the way. When I allowed myself the opportunity to live and learn through the transitions of my life, I gained knowledge that I would not have learned any other way.

Be You-ti-ful means *being true to who you are* and *being true to what you have been assigned or commissioned to do*. You have to learn the lessons that life offers in order to get to a place of being your authentic self.

Walking this path is not easy. There will be things, people, situations, and experiences that you will have to let go of. If you don't, it will cost you everything. If you do, you will gain everything. In other words, if you dare take this journey, "eyes have not seen, nor have ears heard, nor has it even entered into your heart the things God has prepared." Why? Because He loves you, and He wants what's best for you.

You have to go through the Be You-ti-ful journey in order to expand your capacity to receive all that God has. When it hits us the hardest, we lose hope. We lose faith in Him and faith in ourselves to survive. We start to think we don't deserve any more than we have already been through. The devil is a liar! The journey to Be You-ti-ful will require you to ask yourself hard questions. You have to answer these questions with authenticity to get to the truth. Your truth will give you the space to receive because that space will be filled with your willingness to see yourself for who you really are. Just like the lady who was on the subway in the movie Coming To America, "Take a chance, honey."

As you read this book, I am going to ask one thing of you. Be honest with yourself as you read each chapter, each page, each thought. No one is going to judge you or criticize you. When you can be honest with yourself and admit where you are and why you are where you are…that's when you will transition from a cocoon to Be You-ti-ful! Let's go on this journey together. I'll be here with you through every step, through every decision you have to make along the way.

CHAPTER ONE

Be Above It

P icture it. It was December 2013 on a bitter cold Monday night. I stormed out of a meeting, got in my car, and drove off. I was hot! It's one thing to be mad. It's another thing to be hot! My business partner at the time, Craig, who was in the meeting, called me and asked if I was okay. I said, "Uuuuuuh, no! I'm sick and tired of giving and giving and giving, only to not be respected for who I am and what I bring to the table. I deserve to be respected, too!"

Craig said, "I hear what you are saying, and I hear what you are saying."

Now mind you, I was so upset that I couldn't really "hear" what he meant. My response to him was, "What does that mean?" Whatever! (In my Steve Harvey voice, lol.)

"You are too upset to hear me, but when you calm down, you will hear and understand what I am saying."

Today, I clearly understand what he meant.

I remember hearing a quote once that said, "Sometimes you have to get mad enough to change." As a result of that meeting, I had to conclude that "enough was enough." Enough of sacrificing my time, effort, and self-worth for the happiness of others. Enough of neglecting my health, wealth, and well-being just to say that I am loyal. Enough of not going after what God has for me because I'm too busy pushing everybody else to their victory. What I had to realize was that *the only person that I could change was myself.* For others to see your worth and value you, you have to see it, embrace it, and own it yourself. You have to "be above it." You have to see yourself for who you shall be instead of who you settled to become.

I love water! I love to hear the waves. I love to watch sunsets over the ocean. I went on several cruises in college to perform with the Harris Stowe Concert Chorale, and my favorite time was to go and eat at the midnight buffet...and then go to the top deck to listen to the waves. That atmosphere gave me such peace and cleared my thoughts.

Did you know that there are two types of plants that live in the ocean? Plants that have roots will be found on the ocean floor. Plants that don't have roots will be found just drifting on the surface. What I found interesting is that the rooted plants will only be found in shallow water because there is not enough sunlight to sustain them in deep waters. This spoke so clearly to me. If plants need sunlight in order to live, so do we. We need that light, or, as I like to call it, a *revelation*. This revelation teaches us that for us to live the abundant life which is free for us all, we have to create a life for ourselves that promotes God's best for us. Plants can't live without the sun. We can't live without the truth of who we are and why! This will include the good and the bad. We have to live above the lies we have believed about ourselves. We have to live above the mentality that loyalty supersedes you! When you live above it, you are one step closer to the life you deserve.

As a result of that bitter cold December night, I decided to become transparent and share my story, my journey of transitions, and my triumphs with you who are reading. It is my prayer that you who are reading have received this book at a time when there is something in your life that may need change. That something may be you.

My life-changing journey showed me how to become the highest expression of who I am created to be. I had to change who I had conditioned myself into believing. This journey is still teaching me how to live above it all. Live above the disappointments, frustrations, and heartbreaks. Live above poor decisions concerning life and love. The Be You-ti-ful process unveils who you are really created to be. My process has allowed me to share a series of experiences, stories, and lessons that I have learned along the way. For me, some lessons took years to learn, some took weeks, and some took one conversation!

[be you.ti.ful]

#beyoutifulprayerforlivingaboveit

Help me to accept
what I allowed myself
to believe about myself.
Help me to accept
that change starts
the moment I accept it.

CHAPTER TWO

Be Extra

That unforgettable December night was the beginning of my season of transition. I call it a "season" because just like seasons change from winter, spring, summer, and fall, so do the days or seasons of our lives. Different seasons require different armor. In our lives, when seasons change, so should we.

In order to understand the season I was in, I started to study the term "transition." According to Google, the word "transition" means "the process or period of changing, transformation, metamorphosis, or alteration." According to scripture in Ecclesiastes chapter 3 verse 1, it states, "To everything there is a time and season." In 1974, a classic vocalist Benard Ighner sang a captivating song. He used a symphony as his musical backdrop, produced by Quincy Jones, to simply sing, "Everything must change. Nothing stays the same." According to the old hymn of the Baptist church where I grew up, Mt. Zion Baptist Church, "Life is filled with swift transitions." From investigating these resources, I learned a very simple yet complex thought. *Sooner or later, things change! Period.* No matter how hard you work, how much you try to avoid it, how much you try to hide, or how much you try to manipulate.

In order to Be You-ti-ful you have to accept that change starts with you. Nobody is responsible for this but you. If you are like me, I can be a creature of habit. I can do the same thing over and over again without realizing that it may be time to do something different, be something different, or become something different.

A dear friend has a word that she uses all the time when she is referring to someone who is very dramatic, full of needing attention, or just plain loud. She says, "They are so extra!" This kind of person needs so much attention in order to function from day to day. Things that the average person would consider insignificant, an *extra* person deems as being a nightmare. When they enter a room, everyone knows it. Not because they have a presence that commands attention, but because they need attention from others to feel significant. For example, my mother has been a musician, music director, and composer for over sixty years. Many years ago, she was asked to play for a banquet where then-President Bill Clinton was the keynote speaker. I remember talking to her about the event, and she said that President Clinton had such a presence. She talked about how tall he was and how blue his eyes were. She said he was so captivating when he spoke. Okay, so that's *not* the presence I am referring to. An *extra* person has to have things a certain way, or whatever you are asking or needing from them will not happen. When they get upset, instead of talking through an issue, they become loud, disruptive, and disrespectful. They are manipulative. They can make anybody who doesn't know any better believe anything. They are just plain *extra*!

Ask yourself a few questions:

- Are you *extra*?
- Do you have to control people or situations in order to feel validated?
- Do you need people to give you attention because, somewhere along the way, you forgot how to give it to yourself?
- Do you make too much out of little things because, deep down, you are really upset with yourself about something else?

Usually, the person you are lashing out at has nothing to do with what is really going on with you. For many *"extra* people," they have been that way for so long that they don't even realize how they come across to others.

Another dear friend of mine, Ms. Gates, would always say, "People ultimately represent themselves." Do you know what you are sending out to the world if you demand that the word deposits into you what you won't even give to yourself? In order to Be You-ti-ful you have to take responsibility for your emotions and ask yourself thes e questions. Being *extra* will only resort to lost opportunities, lost relationships, lost potential, and ultimately you will lose you.

You are more than a label of being *extra*. I heard a song once with lyrics that said, "there is a king in you." When a king enters a room, they command presence but not out of insecurities. They command presence *because they have confidence in knowing who they are and who they represent*. They don't need you to approve them. They command your respect, but they will be of royalty whether you like it or not! Find that inner king or queen in you. Do the internal work of your soul and clean out the insecurities that cause you to demand from people what you have the ability to give yourself. This is not grammatically correct, but no one wants to babysit your "extra-ness." You are missing out on all the favor, blessings, and peace God has for you. Leave that extra spirit in your past and Be You-ti-ful!

[be you.ti.ful]

#beyoutifulprayerfortheextra

Heal me in places I can't see,
Heal me so my spirit can be free.

CHAPTER THREE

Be Yielding

❝ The long-term effects of knowing too much information is the need to be first." These are the words from academy award-winning actor Denzel Washington. Denzel was referring to the media during the 2016 presidential campaign. Needless to say, the campaign for our next United States President at the time was vicious, but the long-term effects will be felt for quite some time.

There is nothing wrong with acquiring degrees, reading to gain knowledge, and studying a craft. The problem is when you *allow your knowledge to hold you hostage.* When you are so narrow in your perceptions that you have got to be right or you have to be the first in everything, you become pompous. You can miss quality experiences or opportunities due to your need to be the one and only at anything! I am a believer that quality over quantity wins every time.

I've been a teacher for over twenty years now, and I remember when I had to report to a meeting. I prepared for the meeting. I had all of my data, notebook for notes, and pens in hand. I was ready to show that I was a veteran teacher, and I had the mentality…"I got this." Well, when the meeting started, it was clear that I had the wrong data. I needed additional reports. I wasn't even sure where to get the information from. I was completely lost! I was so embarrassed and just mad at myself for thinking I had it all together when actually I was the weakest link. (Remember that game show, lol?)

Having the need to be "first" or be right is a spirit of pride. Do you think that you are the only answer? This can be a dangerous perception. Many times these people won't allow anyone to correct them, and they won't even receive an opinion that is not in line with theirs.

There is someone I know who is an executive administrator like none other. I'll call her Carol. She has an attention to detail and protocol that would make a CEO of a Fortune 500 intimidated. The only thing is she was never wrong. She can tell you what everyone else is not doing, and she can tell you where you are wrong but would not take responsibility for her own shortcomings if you paid her to. I remember having a conference call with her to debrief after a major event we both worked on. Now mind you, I was the coordinator of the event, and she was on staff for the event. It had been brought to my attention that there was a huge oversight that occurred in the planning of the event, and this was "her responsibility." When I spoke to her about this, she refused to take responsibility. She swore that it was not her responsibility. This occurrence caused me to quickly learn that when you are planning or when you are just overseeing anything, don't forget to document, document, document! Anywho, I had the documentation, but she was so full of "herself" that she didn't want to admit the mistake. She even flipped the script and suggested that it was my fault. Now, I did take responsibility for not touching base with her on her responsibilities. I trusted her to get everything done. The thing is, even when you trust someone, you still have to double and sometimes triple-check. That's for any event planners who are reading. As my mother told me once, "Everybody doesn't have the same motives as you."

Being yielding means to be hard, rigid, unwilling to adjust. The Be You-ti-ful concept deals with confronting a hard heart. Have you ever known someone whose heart is cold? No matter what someone says or does, they are just not open to giving or receiving. They can't even accept a compliment.

As teachers, we rise early in the morning. As I progressed during my newfound health and wellness lifestyle, I developed a routine in the mornings. As I arrived at work, focused on getting through my routine, one of the teachers stopped me in my tracks in the hallway. She said, "Ms. Watkins, every time I see you, you are getting smaller and smaller. You look really good." Now, my initial response was going to be, "Oh, well, I'm working at it. It's not easy. I hate working out, especially when I work out early in the morning." Instead of me just accepting her compliment, I immediately went negative. I stopped myself and just simply told her, "Thank you. I really appreciate that."

Being unyielding means allowing God to soften your heart and see the best in any situation. When you have a healed spirit, you can see the best in people. Now, the teacher who complimented me had always been pleasant and gracious, so why would I lessen the value of her words by automatically seeing the worst part of it? When you learn to walk in a spirit of authenticity, you will receive even early in the morning! Your "morning" may not be a time on a clock, but it could be a time or season of your life to embrace a new day, new thought processes, a new identity. When you do this, it will become second nature for you to give and receive.

[be you·ti·ful]

#beyoutifulprayerfortheunyielding

Show me how to give,
Teach me how to receive.

CHAPTER FOUR

Be Observant

For seven years, I served in ministry under an incredible man of God. Being events coordinator, it was my responsibility to oversee the execution of services at our church. We would debrief weekly, and there were times when he would ask me about something that happened during the service. I remember feeling clueless because I had no idea what he was talking about. Little did I know that he didn't miss anything! He had tunnel vision. He could see the most inconspicuous aspects of any service. He would tell me to make sure my team was observant. When you are observant, you see everything. You see what people are saying, what they are doing, and you even have to discern what they haven't done yet.

In your pursuit to Be You-ti-ful there are a few areas of your life that deserve your immediate observation.

When you are on your journey to defining the most authentic version of yourself, *look to observe who is being authentic with you.* Who celebrates you no matter what season you are in? On my way home to write this chapter, I had a conversation with a friend. She was about to publish her first book, and she was a little bothered that one of her friends didn't seem to share her enthusiasm about her newfound success. I listened to her story and said to her, "A real friend will be more excited than you." Now, I am not suggesting that you need a fan club every time you make a decision, but when you are making critical directional changes in your life, pay attention to who shows up and what they do when they get there.

Be observant of who shows up for you. I had surgery to have fibroids removed. My dear friend Rachelle was there the entire time. She even left her job and her husband and kids to be there. When I need encouragement, a laugh, a meal, or the truth, Rachelle is there. Everybody needs a Rachelle!

Be observant as to who conveniently disappears when you need them most. I am not suggesting that relationships are based on what someone can do for you; but what I am saying is, if you need a soft place to land, and who you thought would be there goes MIA, that tells you their ultimate motive. Some can't handle what you are becoming. Your willingness to see yourself for who you really are is intimidating to someone who found strength in your weakness. Walk away from anyone who can't celebrate who you are and who you are becoming. Watch as well as pray.

[be you.ti.ful]

#beyoutifulprayerfortheobservant

Help me to discern who and why.

CHAPTER FIVE

Be Open

Okay, so while I'm writing this book, I am single. It is my prayer and desire to be married and have a family of my own. I have felt this way for years but what I didn't realize was that even though I said I wanted marriage, I wasn't open to love. Many times being closed with our hearts can be a learned behavior. Well, I learned that very well! I was a master at my craft...From the education of children to orchestrating events, I had that! As it relates to matters of the heart, I was closed for business. I knew how to love people from my heart as it related to ministry, but I was terrified of becoming vulnerable with my heart with a man. My heart was so fragile. I was simply scared.

I remember having a huge disagreement with someone I was dating. I felt things should have been further along for us, but they weren't. We had been dating for about seven or eight months. I questioned him and stormed out of his apartment! I was *done!* Now, years later, I can look back and see that anything worth having takes time. I wasn't willing to give us "time." I wasn't willing to be open. Things had to go my way, or I was d-o-n-e! For me, I was in need of controlling what happened and when it happened, or I was *out*. My heart was so fragile. I didn't know how to love from a vulnerable place, so for me, it was easier to walk away rather than take the risk of following my heart.

Be You-ti-ful means being whole enough to be vulnerable or open with the delicate parts of you. When you are whole emotionally, even though you may be uncomfortable being vulnerable, you will walk with an assurance that God will have the final say, and even if your heart is broken, He will restore and position you to receive the love of your life.

Being open also means being open to new experiences. Again, you probably know me pretty well by now, but when it comes to my career and my craft, I am open 24/7. I was ready to explore what could be done. I would push the limits. I would go where no one has ever thought to go. Now, personally, that's a horse of another color. I was so narrow in my scope of myself that the thought of trying something new or unusual for me was just not optional.

I was a horrible cook! I would cook it, burn it, and then I was over it! I wasn't consistent enough to become good at it. I remember trying to cook for my family once. They were gracious, but it didn't turn out well. I'm so glad I picked up some chicken instead of frying it that time! I was so frustrated and embarrassed. What I didn't realize was I was attempting to cook and prepare a meal the way I thought they wanted it instead of exploring what type of cooking techniques and dishes I could handle. See, when you are open to new experiences, you still have to stay true to you. If you try to become something you are not, it will only end in disaster or a horrible beef roast!

Be open to embracing new people in your life. I'm not suggesting to let any and everybody into your personal space, but I am suggesting that you become a more well-rounded person when you can embrace people from all walks of life. I truly believe that the people you attract are a direct reflection of you!

Have you heard of the story between Ruth and Boaz? Any single person reading this has…I'm sure. Boaz was a wealthy landowner. According to scripture, Ruth was busy tending to the fields when Boaz saw her. I'm sure Boaz was physically attracted to Ruth, but in order for a Boaz (a King) to meet you where you are, he has to see himself somewhere in you. He has to see his heart, his work ethic, his light. Ruth made a covenant to Naomi that she would not leave her after the death of both of their husbands. Now tell me Boaz didn't discern her heart.

If you find yourself attracting the same kind of people into your life, *check your own heart*. Check your own character, and it will tell you everything you need to know about the other person and you.

I remember having a huge event some time ago. I literally created this event from the ground up. I solicited the help of my family and close friends. Mistaken assumption number 1: "everybody is not going to support your efforts, even if you supported theirs." I was enormously disappointed when a very dear friend at the time did not come through the way I thought she would. To me, we had assisted each other in so many of our previous endeavors, so I just knew she would do the same in return. Not so! I tried to reach out and talk to her about it, but for some reason, she wasn't quick to make herself available. I couldn't understand what was happening. I decided to drop it and just let it be. What I came to realize was that what she did was a direct reflection of what I had done to myself for years. When I needed to be there for "myself," I wasn't. When I needed to put myself first and do what was best for me, I didn't. I was too consumed with protecting my pride instead of recognizing that pride came right before a mighty fall. I had to forgive myself for what I had allowed in my own life. *You can't get mad when people treat you the way you treat yourself.* As a result of coming into my own truth, I had an assurance that once I developed a healthier view of who I was and what I needed to produce for my life, I would attract people who would do the same. From that point on, I started to attract genuine people who offered true relationships.

Oh, by the way, that event also confirmed yet again who my real friends were. My friend Toni was so sick, couldn't talk because she was so hoarse, and she still went over and beyond as my party planner. Another friend got a babysitter for her three kids just to come. Remember, your friends are a reflection of you.

[be you·ti·ful]

In the spring of 2016, I had a series of dizzy spells. I went to see my doctor, and she suggested a hysterectomy. Mind you, I came to accept the hysterectomy. I was very distraught. I didn't get a second opinion. I didn't even ask God if this was His will. I just settled for what I was told. (That's the next book…)

One evening I was at work late, and I ran into our counselor Mrs. Steele-Starks. We started chatting, and I told her what the doctor conveyed. She looked at me and said emphatically, "Don't do that." She gave me the name of Dr. Simckes and said, "Call him!" I called and made an appointment. I went to see him. He looked at my charts and said, "These fibroids can be removed without a hysterectomy." I was done! Now, Dr. Simckes is one of the top fertility specialists in the country, and his office was *five minutes* from my apartment!

Well, fast forward three months later, and I was in the recovery room when I woke up after surgery. Dr. Simckes came in and said, "You made me work today." (He's a comedian too…lol.) "I had to remove twenty-five fibroids from you! This was a delicate procedure, and I had to remove them two-three at a time. You had little to no blood loss. You didn't even need to go into intensive care. You are a lucky young lady." Be You-ti-ful means *making sure your spirit is clear so you can be open to who God will use to bless you.* Dr. Simckes saved my life.

This chapter has focused on being open. In order to be open, you have to also be open to a new level of giving. In a previous season, if there was a TV character that would describe me, it would have been Olivia Pope. She and I were "fixers." I gave what I had. I gave what I didn't have. I saw a problem, and I solved it. I would stay up for nights to create a solution. I thought you showed love by giving. That's true, but you can't give to the point of neglecting all the things that make you unique. Now when I was the fixer, I had no idea that the level of sacrifice that I gave in a previous season would be reciprocated through Dr. Simckes.

In order to Be You-ti-ful you have to *be open to receiving from people and life circumstances through a new level of giving.* A new level of giving means accepting people who want to make a deposit in your life that goes beyond what you have the ability to give to yourself. So many times we say "I'm good" when you know you are not because you don't want to be vulnerable. Look what happened when I became vulnerable and opened up to Mrs. Steele-Starks!

To some, vulnerable equals weak. To me, vulnerability represents strength. To suggest that I do need help or I don't have it all together is a sign of maturity. It illustrates that you can "own" your "stuff" and still be okay. You can declare that God still has a purpose and plan for your life. You still have a destiny.

On YouTube, I saw an artist by the name of Tim Bowman. He has a video that I am in love with titled "I'm Good." Here are a few lyrics:

I'm Good
Good enough to love myself,
Good enough to have success;
What you gain from all your stress
Is the freedom to know
that you are blessed.
Good enough to handle my biz,
Good enough to raise my kids;
The past is the past,
And honestly,
I'm happy
for where I'm
because
I'm good.

[be you.ti.ful]

#beyoutifulprayertobeopen

Help me to see you, God,
through my vulnerability.
Once I see you
I'm good.

CHAPTER SIX

Be Uncompromising

As I began writing this chapter, my heart is filled with much joy and sadness. Four days ago, family and friends laid to rest my dear friend, mentor, and mother figure Erma Gates. She would be pleased as punch (one of her favorite sayings) that I'm including her in this book. Ms. Gates had a personality that was larger than life. She had quick wit and wisdom that was priceless. I remember when Ms. Gates decided to have a dinner party for her close friends. First of all, she was a premier party planner. She created the menu, décor, guest list, and entertainment. She stayed on my head to make sure I was on time! When I arrived, she was busy setting everything up. Every single detail had to be in a certain place. I decided to set up the punch bowl for her, but she said, "No, it belongs over there." I didn't really see what the big deal was, but for her, she had a vision, and she was not going to compromise on what she had in mind for her party. Someone else coming into her space was not going to change what her vision was! I hope you know where I'm going with this.

To Be You-ti-ful, you have to have an *uncompromising spirit*. Nothing and no one should alter what you know God has spoken into your spirit. This has to be your mantra, even as it relates to dating and relationships.

There are some who believe in old fashion romance and others who believe this no longer exists. One of my favorite movies of all times is a film called *The Mirror Has Two Faces*. This is a Barbra Streisand picture. Barbra's character Rose was a very popular college professor who was close to fifty and still living with her mother. Her students loved her, but she looked twenty years older than she was. Her clothes were twice her size, and she never went out. Through a series of events, Rose met another very nice-looking college professor, and they began a friendship. He decided that sexual relationships complicated a bond between a man and a woman. She was so drawn to him that she decided to marry him with the agreement that they would not have sex. (Okay, I'm going to let you breathe on that.) Well, when she finally "asked" if they could have sex, he got so upset and said she was not who he thought she was.

Well, after getting over her broken heart, this college professor realized that she settled for what she really didn't want. She wanted the romance of it all! She thought that his concept of love and relationships was just plain "crazy." Well, after she forgave herself for agreeing to what she really didn't want and recognized who SHE was, which was an intelligent, sophisticated woman, she took a leave of absence from her job and worked on herself. *Remember this, a broken heart many times is the doorway to finding you.* After her break up, she got a makeover, lost 30 pounds, and looked gorgeous. Now, of course, this is a movie. When her love interest realized how absolutely foolish he had been, he raced to her house, made a complete fool out of himself, and admitted that he was so afraid of being rejected that he created a false sense of security. She thought that it was her fault that he didn't want her. Remember this too; *many times, when someone rejects you, it's because they rejected themselves first.*

Now, I'm no Barbra Streisand, but after all these years of living and not fully understanding why I have yet to find the "one," I can clearly see that a man cannot give you what he doesn't already have, and you cannot receive what you aren't willing to stand for. Being uncompromising also means never to settle. *Ever!* There is a certain level of sacrifice in any relationship, but don't waver on your morals, values, and the compass of your soul.

I remember rekindling an old flame years ago. I was so enamored by him. He had the swag, the look, the conversation, and a spiritual gift that was beyond anything I had ever seen. We talked, and texted, and talked. I was convinced that he was going to be "the one." I was so consumed with him that his character flaws, lack of integrity in his private life, and a total disregard of spiritual convictions never occurred to me until all of this was brought to the surface. That was a come-to-Jesus light bulb moment for me. I clearly heard God say to me, "It's either him or me. You can't have both."

I'm going to be very honest with you. It was not easy to sever ties with him. I had gotten very used to him being a part of my daily life, but I had to let him go. I considered him to be a blessing in one season of my life. However, in order for me to embrace and receive the full scope of my destiny, I had to realize that he was not good for me during this part of my journey. Our value systems were very different. I started to think that because I had a spirit of "fear," I could not accept who he was and what he believed in.

The truth of the matter is there is a difference between fear and reverence. My covenant with God just would not allow me to submit to his way of living and moving in the world. *Remember this as well: how someone else chooses to live their life does not have to be how you choose to live yours.* Just like Rose, after I got over my heartbreak, I picked up the pieces and focused on myself. Soon after, my life took off. *Literally!* God positioned me to receive what I never thought would have ever been possible for myself. Due to the lessons I learned, I can now walk in my truth and become what I want to attract and who I want to attract. Who or what has you bound? Where have you settled? Today is a good day to live again like Rose and like me.

Did you know that Louis Vuitton products never go on sale? A man by the name Henri Recamier married into the Vuitton family and was the first outsider to take over the business. He discovered a system known as vertical integration. This system dates back to the 1970s.

According to author Sarah Schmalbruch from businessinsider. com, this is what Recamier did next:

> Recamier noticed that retailers who sold Vuitton products were marking up the bags by at least 100 percent, putting all the profits in their pockets and leaving little money for the manufacturers. Recamier came up with a solution. Nixing that greedy retail middleman—in other words, opening wholly-owned stores or controlling concessions—would mean Vuitton could keep that money for himself. So that's what Recamier did. His move doubled profit margins overnight: as conventional luxury firms remained at the traditional 15 to 20 percent, his reinvented company hit 40 percent or more.

According to author Mark Ellwood, vertical integration meant that Vuitton not only owned its own factories, but the company also leased the space it uses for the LV mini boutiques you see on the selling floor of various department stores.

Therefore, Vuitton can control the actual manufacturing of its products (if a certain handbag isn't selling, it can decrease production of that handbag), and it can staff and operate those mini boutiques directly. So LV never sells its products wholesale to a department store, which means the department store can't sell LV's products for a sale price.

What this says to me is you can control who steps to you, ladies, based on the price tag you put on yourself. If you keep attracting the same type of spirit into your life, you may want to decrease the production of your availability. If he wants your attention, then he will have the currency or the integrity to afford you. This goes for business deals, healing broken family relationships, or even entertaining a new friend.

The price you put on yourself will determine who can afford you. You are not meant to go on sale. You are not meant to be a discount. You are too valuable to settle for what someone else is willing to pay. You are worth the full price.

[be you.ti.ful]

#beyoutifulprayerforanuncompromisingspirit

I'm not for sale,
Teach me to know that
I am enough.

CHAPTER SEVEN

Be Sensitive

The most dangerous storms happen when seasons are changing. According to www.wikipedia.com, the Atlantic hurricane season is the period in a year from June through November when hurricanes usually form in the Atlantic Ocean. Tropical cyclones in the North Atlantic are called hurricanes, tropical storms. The strongest time for hurricane activity seems to be between mid-August through mid-October or between summer and fall.

I lived in the Midwest for over forty years, and everyone bunkers down when winter is about to change to spring. We are known for having earth-shattering tornadoes, hail the size of snowballs, and lightning that lights up a midnight sky. Most damage takes place in between seasons.

My dear friend Pastor Raphaelle is an incredible playwright. She wrote a stage play production titled *Seasons*. She tells a story of a woman who walks through the seasons of her life. She experiences the death of a husband, raising children, making ends meet, developing authentic friendships, recognizing that death is a part of life, and how our hope is always in our Lord and Savior Jesus Christ. Pastor Raphaelle wrote a song that I want to use as the foundation to this chapter. Her words are, "Be sensitive to your season…which season are you in?"

In order to be sensitive to your season, you have to recognize when your season is changing. What is going on in your life that is making a mandate for you to change? Like I mentioned a moment ago, when seasons change, the weather can be unpredictable, dangerous, and at times the weather forecasters can't make sense of what's happening. In our daily lives, we can use these same principles. Have you ever experienced a situation that just didn't make sense? Someone's behavior or even your behavior, decisions, or circumstances just didn't add up? No matter how you flipped this situation in your thinking, you couldn't figure out what happened and why.

If you have ever found yourself in this stage in life, please let me be the first to tell you that your seasons are changing. You are in transition. Either something needs to change, or you need to change. I know that's a hard pill to swallow. When someone else's behavior shifts or violates you, how is it that *you* have to change? Well, I'm glad you asked. This leads to the next step in this process. You have to start asking yourself more hard questions.

Asking yourself hard questions will not be easy. This process will cause you to have to be honest with yourself. You will have to be able to take responsibility for your part of any situation. Now you may say, "I didn't do anything wrong! *They* violated *me!*" Taking responsibility means owning the fact that this happened to you. It means admitting it to yourself instead of acting as if it didn't exist. It means being set free from the residue from it.

Take some time and ask yourself the following questions:

- What happened that you just don't understand?
- Who was involved and why?
- What is this situation saying to you about you? About them?
- How did this situation or the effects of this situation change you?
- What do you need to change or do differently?
- Why?
- What will life be like once you make this change?
- Who can be your accountability while you are walking through this change?

Once you are able to answer these questions, *breathe*. This is a complex request, but it is necessary. When you breathe, you take in new air. You need air to live. The new air of your truth is what you will need in order to live again. Many times we stop living and start existing when we don't deal with traumatic or unexplainable seasons in life.

There is one last thing you have to do once you have asked and answered hard questions. You must *move!* This may or may not be a geographical move. This may be a spiritual move. This may be a natural move. This may even be an emotional move.

You can't expect long-lasting change if you are not willing to get out of your comfort zone. On your mark…get set…move!

[be you.ti.ful]

#beyoutifulprayertobesensitive

*Help me to know
what season I am in,
Give me the power to move.*

CHAPTER EIGHT

Be Innocent

I remember when my nephew CJ was about three years old. One day he discovered the art of the telephone. He called me at least twenty times in one day. I would say "Hello," and he would just laugh hysterically and then hang up! To hear a three-year-old laugh is so precious! Now even though we are far from children, I submit to you that as you navigate through this season, you may have to reverse your mentality and delve back to a "child-like state." I'm not suggesting that you lose the ability to be a mature adult with responsibilities, but as we become adults, we have to recognize that we were simply taught wrong in some areas of our lives.

Many times our parents teach us with fear and trembling in order for us to survive. We are taught to get a job with benefits! We are taught to look good! We are taught to use our gifts and talents to the glory of God! There is absolutely nothing wrong with that! We, as children of God, are servants. Servants serve! What I *am* suggesting is there are some areas of our lives that were not cultivated. There were no seeds planted. You can't expect a harvest if there was not a seed planted. Everything starts with a seed.

For me, as I began my transitional season, I really felt like a child in a candy store. I felt like my eyes were finally open to what life really could consist of. I was so consumed with working on my career or in ministry that I was not living. I was merely existing. I was so afraid of making a mistake or being wrong that I wouldn't do anything. I want to be married, but I wasn't even open to dating in a healthy manner. Now, I'm not saying that you should go out with anybody who's interested, but you at least need to know what you like or what you don't like.

For example, about four years ago, I met someone for breakfast. We set a time to get together at IHOP. (By the way, I love pancakes!) I arrived and sat, and sat, and sat, and waited, and waited, and waited. Almost an hour later, he called and said he overslept and was on the way. I could have left, and I would have been within my right, but I stayed. Okay, so he was already an hour late, but then this joker (sorry...pray for me...lol) walked in with sweatpants and a T-shirt full of grease spots. Now, by this time, I was like, "Really?" That was an indication that this breakfast was officially over. He began to talk about how most women want a man's money and not them. *Sir, we are at IHOP, so how you figured that I wanted your money is beyond me.*

This chapter is not necessarily about dating, but I wanted to use this example to illustrate a valuable point. As I left IHOP, the Holy Spirit asked me a few questions: "Are you ready to do what it takes to prepare for who I have for you? Are you willing to pay the price?" Please notice that God did not ask me one thing about my "date." The Holy Spirit will use your experiences to get your undivided attention.

So, what does this have to do with innocence? Once I answered the questions with "Yes," I began a time in my life unlike any other. I was always so focused on *who I wanted* that I neglected to become *what I wanted.*

Children grow up by walking, talking, eating, and listening. If you observe a child long enough, whatever is in them naturally comes out. They have parents or those who have the heart of a parent to cultivate their development. Anybody can have a child, but not everyone is a parent.

At the same token, I became like a child again. I sat under people who could cultivate in me what it means to be a wife. Mrs. Williams was the school secretary when I taught second grade. She is also a pastor's wife. I remember going to dinner with her, and she began to talk to me about how she and her husband communicate. After about two hours, we were about to leave, and she said, "Wait a minute, Sylvia. Let me check to make sure I have my grocery list. I have to pick up a few things for dinner. You see, my ministry is him. He ministers to God's people, and I minister to him." I was completely blown away. So, you mean to tell me when you have a mate, they become your ministry? Do you mean to tell me that they are your priority? So for real, you mean to tell me I have to become the kind of woman who can submit my strength in order to meet the needs of my husband. So I have to become a wife *now*? While I'm *single*, I have to become a wife? Now that's a revelation!

Now, for some of you, marriage is not your calling, and I'm not suggesting it should be. However, what I am saying is that in order for you to become Be You-ti-ful you have to *sit under a mentor and learn*. Somewhere along the line, we have missed the power of being taught. What we have done is become our own teacher. We believe our own counsel. We believe that if we read, study, or obtain enough knowledge, we don't need to submit to someone who has walked where you are trying to walk. Or, what we do is find a mentor, but we only take the information that we are comfortable with. Anything that requires us to change our behavior or perception we reject. Just like a child, a parent can tell a child to not touch a hot stove, but due to the curiosity of children, they have to touch the stove, get burned, and holler until the walls cave in order for them to learn how to listen!

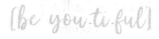

At the same time, in order to gain this innocence, you have to rid yourself of emotionally toxic people. We are no better than the people we surround ourselves with. How do you define emotionally toxic? Anything that is toxic is poisonous. It's a substance that eats at the fiber of any area of exposure that it has access to. An emotionally toxic person studies your areas of brokenness, vulnerabilities, esteem deficiencies, and lack. They lead you into a time of healing. You may even think they are really for you. Emotionally toxic perpetrators are a student of their prey. They know what you want to hear, how you want to feel, what you've longed for. Please hear me when I say this. When you don't know the level of your broken state, you will be the subject of emotionally toxic predators. When a toxic substance enters a naive open vessel, that vessel has no idea of the damage it will cause. The vessel will reject it, and the unwanted waste will dispose of itself in various ways. (You know what I mean…) When you are experiencing an emotionally toxic person, it will affect every area of your life. Your attitude shifts. What used to bring you joy you stray away from. You distanced yourself from relationships and people who love you and want what's best for you. This is a spirit that is attacking the core of who you really are and who God has called you to be. If you continue to embrace toxic people, it will literally make you sick. It will taint your thoughts, perceptions, and actions. You will believe their voice over your own. Get rid of emotionally toxic people. Protect your innocence today!

Have you ever noticed that some children can play by themselves? They don't need a playdate. They don't need a best buddy. They can take crayons, pencils, or blocks and play for hours using their imagination. These unique children have such a spirit of peace when they are alone. Nothing bothers them. Nothing disturbs them. They don't even say, "Mama, I'm hungry" for a good two or three hours!

During your season of developing your innocence, you will have a need to create your own peace. Once I got settled into my apartment back in St. Louis, I would work on this book for hours in complete silence. Now honestly, after teaching a classroom full of eight-year-olds all day, I enjoyed the silence.

I started to pay attention to who was in my personal space. I have a very dear friend Masa. We have the type of friendship where we don't talk all the time, but when we talk or do a girls' day, it is always so peaceful. Masa carries a tranquil spirit. It's not that life does not affect her; it's just that she has learned to allow the peace of God that surpasses all understanding to guard her heart and mind. Having those kinds of people in my inner circle is crucial to Be You-ti-ful. Your destiny will be fed by the people you surround yourself with.

I recognize that developing an innocent spirit is not as easy as it seems. For those who are used to being in control of everything and everyone, this may seem to be impossible. Being innocent means you have to admit that you don't know it all. You may not even know what's really best for you in this new season. This causes vulnerability that may be unfamiliar. Dare to believe that your innocence will be covered by God and will lead to a newfound freedom in who you are and who you shall be.

(be you.ti.ful)

#beyoutifulprayerfortheinnocent

*Help me to understand
that my innocence is a
protected doorway.*

CHAPTER NINE

Be Free to Fall Forward

One of my all-time favorite preachers is Bishop T.D. Jakes. He has a sermon called "Overcoming Silent Frustrations." This is a prophetic declaration to anyone who is ready for change in their life but struggles with what you never speak about. In this sermon, he said, "Sometimes failure is a relief because at least you know where you stand."

Prior to hearing this word, I associated failure as defeat. I would always associate failure as being final. It never occurred to me that failure may be the reality of the moment, but it is not the conclusion of the matter. When life situations or circumstances happen to me, there are a few things that I have found that work in order to "fall forward." Falling forward means that even though you missed the mark or made a detrimental mistake, you can still learn from it and move on.

I heard Oprah say once that there are really no mistakes in life. When circumstances don't work out the way we thought or we miss the mark, just know that these situations only place you closer to where you are really supposed to be. There is no failure, just steps to get us closer to our next.

Here are a few helpful hints if you battle with the spirit of failure. (Another TD Jakes classic; Youtube this one too!)

[be·you·ti·ful]

Own It

When I taught second grade, I enjoyed them so much. They were quite comical at times. In order for my students to own some of their poor decision-making, I would allow the class to correct an issue they saw. If someone made a poor choice, I would ask the entire class, "Why did they do that?" Due to the fact that kids love to expose the truth, everyone would say the guilty party's name and why they thought the incident happened. Now, because the student in question has twenty pairs of eyes looking at them, they would go ahead and admit their guilt. We would talk about it as a class. I would ask the class to give the "suspect in question" advice as to what they can do differently, and we would move on with the rest of our day.

Just like my delightful students, we must learn to take ownership of our part of any situation. Now, you won't have a class full of second graders looking at you, but you will have your past looking at you. Your past will try to haunt your spirit into thinking that you either deserved the consequences of your behavior or that you can't get past it. Matthew 5:25 says *agree with the adversary quickly*. I say own your stuff quickly. When you prolong taking ownership of your issue, lack of wisdom, or poor decision making, you deny our God the ability to begin the healing process in your life. Just like a natural wound on your body, remember that healing takes time.

I had major surgery in the summer of 2016. I was on bed rest for the entire summer! Yes, the *entire summer!* When I first came home from the hospital, it took me at least thirty minutes to sit up in the bed, roll to the edge of the bed, get up, walk to the bathroom, sit down, get up again, walk back to the bed, sit down, lay down and get comfortable! The beauty in this situation was that each day, little by little, step by step, it got a little easier. I remember going to the doctor for a check-up. I told him it seemed as if it was taking forever for me to get back to normal. He said something I will never forget: "You have to stop fighting the healing and accept that it will take time for your body to heal. Healing from the inside takes time, and only your body knows how long that will take."

If you are reading these words, I pray that you own or accept that healing takes time. Your emotional, psychological, and mental stability will only become whole again once you accept the fact that whatever you are facing actually happened. Many people have this saying of "just get over it." I don't care for that terminology because everyone's timeline for getting over anything is different. However, I guarantee you that once you take responsibility for your part in your healing, your road to healing and wholeness will be enlightened by the light of your acceptance. Remember that your future is waiting on you.

[be you-ti-ful]

Reset

I had an incredible personal trainer Joey. I so appreciate him and his wife for leading me on my health and wellness journey. Joey is a very intense trainer. We workout in the gym. We use the equipment, but many times he uses unconventional ways to workout certain areas. I am a very analytical person. I can mentally analyze a situation forever! I am learning to just let things go. Many times Joey would give me a new exercise. There were times when I would get so frustrated because I couldn't figure out how to do it. I needed it to make sense. He would often tell me to "reset." What he meant was stop, focus, address your misconceptions, and try it again.

When you are overcoming your failures many times, you have to reset. So, the question is, how do you reset?

The first thing you have to do is simply *stop!* Stop believing the lie you are telling yourself that your failure is the end of you. Next, you have to *address misconceptions.* Misconceptions are the thoughts you believe that are in direct contradiction of who you are as a child of our Lord and Savior. After you accept what has happened, *forgive yourself* for what you are saying to yourself about yourself. The enemy is very manipulative. That spirit will have you believe that what you did or what you refused to do makes you scared or unwilling to move forward.

Many times misconceptions are a result of being taught incorrectly due to the dysfunctions of your past. Our parents did the best they knew to do. It took me years to acknowledge that. At the same time, just because they did the best they knew how to do does not mean that you got what you needed. You have to identify these areas of misconceptions.

In education, we teach our students to synthesize. This is a reading strategy we teach in order to get students to deepen their understanding of a story or book. We force them to change their thoughts concerning a book. They will read a book, complete a graphic organizer, and turn and talk to their neighbor about the book. Many times what a student thinks about a book will change by the time they finish their activities. This is what it means to reset. Once you pay the price to do the work and you can recognize how your perceptions were clouded by poor teaching from the past, you are well on your way!

Move On

So okay, you have finally gotten to the end of this chapter. I hope you don't think that's the end of the story. You have done the work to own your stuff. You have made a conscious decision to reset your misconception. So now what? Well, I'm glad you asked. You are finally in a position to move on. When you move on, you can say to yourself what you want and what you don't want. You can say what you need and what you don't need. You can conclude what works for you and what doesn't work for you.

What I am suggesting is that you are entering into what I like to call a "selfish season." Now, for years I thought it was a holy sin to put yourself first. I thought because I am a servant of God that I should be second, third, or (for me) at the bottom of the list. Only until I laid in a hospital bed after having twenty-five fibroids removed without a blood transfusion or being placed in intensive care did I recognize that something had to change. That something was *me*.

Life has a way of waking you up to setting new goals for yourself. As I recovered from that surgery for three months, I took that time to set new goals for myself. I made a list. Hear me when I say this: when you have a made-up mind, you can do anything. I was determined to never allow myself to get to the point where I wasn't taking care of myself. I would never allow someone else's opinion to dictate what I believed about myself. I would never settle! Hear me again: never, ever, settle!

When you fall forward, you learn from your past and keep it moving. From that summer of recovery until now, my life has not been the same. Do I have to remind myself of my deliverance? Yes! Did I find myself going back to my old mental conversations and behaviors at times? Yes!

Anytime I found myself in those states just like the prodigal son, I had to "come to myself." In Luke 15: 17-20, the prodigal son came to himself when he recognized that he was living beneath his birthright. I implore you to "come to yourself." Remind yourself of who you are. Remind yourself of your status as being of a royal priesthood. Declare what your future shall be! Rise up and walk in your God-given authority. Don't allow yourself to be so afraid of failure that you won't even try.

When a baby is learning to walk, it will fall time and time again. The thing I love about babies is their resilience. They always get back up. And when they get up, there is always someone cheering them on! Make sure you have people in your world who only want what's best for you. People that want what's best for you will encourage you when you fall and push you to get up. They will force you to go further than you have gone before. They have no hidden agendas. All they want is for you to go after what's rightfully yours.

As you dare to fall forward, it will take everything you have to do it! You cannot focus on anything other than what lies ahead. This is a do-or-die situation. You have to suffer all to get this. You have to forsake all for this victory. Your entire life has been held up because of this moment. Your breakthrough was delayed until you came to this defining moment and made an intentional decision to do you the way God ordained you to. You may be shaking in your 5 inches or your Jordan's, but I dare you to take this jump! I challenge you to jump afraid. You may jump and not know for sure where you will land but remember this. "Now unto him who is able to keep you from falling and present you faultless before the only wise God our savior, dominion, and power forever and ever" (Jude 24-25). Now you are ready to move on!

[be you.ti.ful]

#beyoutifulprayertofallforward

*Help me to have the courage to
learn what I need to learn
so I can fall forward.*

CHAPTER TEN

Be Undeniable

I remember when my father passed away over twenty years ago. Some of my friends had never seen him before. At the funeral, it was time for the viewing, and a friend of mine came around to view. Not that there should be anything to laugh about at a funeral, but when she came around for the viewing, she looked in the casket and looked at me with her mouth and eyes wide open. Needless to say, I knew why she responded like that, and we both fell out laughing! Here's the thing, I am my father's twin as it relates to what I look like. My father was close to six feet tall, and at his heaviest, he was over 350 pounds. It is undeniable that I look like my father and sound like my mother.

Just like my resemblance to my father, once you have gone through your Be You-ti-ful journey, there is one thing that can no longer be denied. Your emotional freedom, your sense of purpose, your belief in yourself, your commitment to your destiny, and the belief that the best is still yet to come will be like sunshine that glows after a thunderstorm. In order to get to this place, you can no longer deny yourself. So many times, we deny ourselves our own voice.

I remember a meeting I had as I was stepping down from a seven-year tenure as events coordinator and fifteen years as a member of my former church. One of the hardest conversations I ever had was with Bishop. I stepped down and decided I needed to move on in order to find my voice. As an events coordinator, I was responsible for being the voice of the vision of the house. I led a team of incredible women. We were responsible for creating events and developing an atmosphere for people to experience God. Lives were changed, and God was being glorified. After years of this kind of work, my mind, body, and eventually, my soul were tired. In addition to my work as events director, I had a career as a public school educator. The face of education had drastically shifted, and only the grace of God carried me through.

My entire life, even before taking on being an events coordinator, I represented the voice for others. The problem with that was I completely lost myself in the process. I didn't know who I was. I was forty-two years old, gifted, talented, and lost. I didn't know what I wanted, what I liked, or what I desired and how to get it. My voice had been on mute for years.

Finding your voice will require you to have hard conversations based on the decisions you made during your season of personal drought. In these conversations, you have to submit to what you allowed. You cannot blame anyone for what you allowed to happen. People will take what you give them. I did not know myself enough to know what boundaries to set. You have to know what you can and cannot handle. When you find your voice, you find your power. Your power is the thing in you that validates your esteem. Once you find your voice, you will no longer have the capacity to deny you.

Being undeniable also means living without doubt. Anytime you doubt yourself, you learn how to talk yourself out of what you can accomplish. You have to be very careful about what you say and think to yourself because out of the heart, the mouth speaks. You also have to be careful about who you allow to speak into your life because their words will have power over you if you don't trust you.

I recently listened to an interview online. It was an interview with the legendary R&B diva herself, Mary J. Blige. She was on the radio show The Breakfast Club. If you don't know about them, The Breakfast Club, this is a no-holds bar show that uses transparency and today's pop culture's language to raise awareness on what's trending. This interview with Mary J was the most transparent I had ever heard her speak. Her music speaks for itself, but she really opened up about her personal life.

At the time of this interview, she was in the midst of going through a divorce. Their story started out like a love story in a dream. Mary came out of years of failed relationships, abuse, and a series of poor decisions that diminished the value of who she really was. She talked about how her husband would "chip away" at her self-esteem by repeatedly verbalizing her insecurities, wounded areas of her life, and even began to put doubt in her spirit that her fans didn't love her anymore and that she was a "has-been." Well, the host of The Breakfast Club almost lost it when she mentioned this. They questioned how she could allow such a man to do that to her. They talked about how she is the Queen of R&B and how she is timeless, and how her fan base would always love her. Her response to them was chilling. She plainly said, "I loved him, and I was willing to do whatever it took to save my marriage."

I was completely in disbelief by her comments. To look at the stats, Mary has sold over 50 million records. She has had nine number-one hits. Out of all of her career accomplishments and out of the millions of people across this world who completely adore her, she allowed one person to completely strip her of her dignity and destroy her view of herself while placing a spirit of doubt of her ability to continue to change the face of the most revered genre of music R&B! The question then becomes, why would she allow this? Why did she succumb to this treatment? Well, the enemy comes to kill, steal, and destroy. The enemy will use whomever he can gain access to in order to deposit a spirit of doubt based on what you know you have been called to do.

Now, I am in no way discrediting Mary J by any means. I believe that if she can learn the lessons from this horrible treatment in her marriage, she will learn how to embrace who she really is as a woman and artist. She will come out stronger, better, and wiser. She will attract love that is attracted to the authenticity of her wholeness and not someone who capitalizes on her weaknesses or vulnerability. Then, she will produce a record that will supersede any of her award-winning projects thus far because it will speak to her newfound sense of empowerment. I can't wait!

In order to live beyond doubt, you have to govern who you are in covenant with. This could be marriage, friendship, dating, and even family. Covenant relationships should motivate you to become the greatest expression of who you are. Ask yourself this question: do your current covenant relationships drive you toward or away from your authentic self? I heard Iyanla say once to someone on her hit show Iyanla Fix My Life, "People should deserve the classification of being called your friend." That statement was so powerful to me. Anyone in your life who does not prove to you that they should have a seat at your table does not belong there. Period!

When you learn how to live beyond doubt, your table will only be surrounded with people who will sit down and eat at the table with you and then tell you to finish eating while they clean up for you. It's not that you need people to do things for you, but people who are "for you" will want to do whatever they can to usher you into your rest, your peace, or your next move.

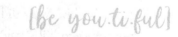

Right in the heat of my transitional time, I remember covering a Donald Lawrence concert for the radio station I was with at the time. I was having a very difficult time personally but was determined to press my way through. Donald Lawrence is, by far, in my opinion, one of the greatest songwriters, producers, and also just a genuine spirit. In the midst of his concert, he sang a song I had never heard before. Here are some of the lyrics:

> And when people ask
> What you're going to do
> With what you know
> God has called you to do
> Just say
> I'm not making sense
> I'm making faith

Now, just let those lyrics sit right there for a few moments. When your process is being questioned, that's a form of planting a seed of doubt. You have to learn how to live beyond questions. You can miss authentic experiences and relationships when you absorb questions about every single move you make. I'm not suggesting that you should not have a discerning spirit, but if you internalize everything, you are only exposing the spirit of fear and insecurity you have. Fear can keep you from the joys of life, and then you become a prisoner to your own emotions. When you decide to live beyond questions, you discover a faith in God like you've never experienced. The decisions you make may not make sense to everyone but just know you are making faith, honey! You will also discover a side of yourself that's been waiting to be set free from the cage you put yourself in.

Once you accept that process of not being denied, living beyond doubt, living beyond questions, then you are ready for the manifestation of what God has for you. Your heart is now open. Your spirit is no longer in captivity to your fears. Then you can let go of those not for you. This will usher in the promises of God for your life. You will then be an undeniable force to the kingdom of God, your family, friends, your circle, and ultimately yourself.

[be you.ti.ful]

#beyoutifulprayerfortheundeniable

Help me to not deny myself,
Help me to make faith.

CHAPTER ELEVEN

Be In Love

I am a hopeless romantic! I admit it. The Hallmark Channel or any romantic comedy is it for me. My BFF Shamika and I have to unpack every love story on the big screen. If you haven't watched the movie The Photograph…it's a must-see! Now true enough, the movies on the Hallmark Channel can be predictable. I can tell within the first five minutes if I will like the storyline and what it will be about. Two people meet. There is unspoken chemistry. They start falling in love. Will they admit their love for each other? Just when you think they will be together, there is an unexpected twist in the story. Will they make it? They finally give in to their love, and in the last thirty seconds of the movie, they have the big kiss. The final credits roll, and you are left with the hope of having your own big kiss. I know that some of you are not here for it. I get it, but I am!

I remember dating this guy once who told me that romance was unrealistic and that it was all in my head. Now, true enough, I had to get my head out of the clouds, but I believe his opinion was based on him planting seeds of what I should not expect from him. But that's my next book! Anyway, life happens, and this can prohibit romance every second of every day. I do, however, believe that love, romance, and the big kiss can be moments in time that can color the pages of our lives.

Now, what do the Hallmark Channel's holiday love marathons have to do with Be You-ti-ful? Have you ever thought about how to be in love with you?

At the beginning of any love story movie, there is always music. This music puts you in the mood for what is to come. Usually, the music is light-hearted yet mysterious. You are looking forward to the movie, but you are already questioning what's going to happen. In order to be in love with you, ask yourself, *what am I listening to?* Music has a way of creating a mood for our days. As a teacher for over twenty-three years, I have been to a lot of places and met all kinds (love lyrics from Donald Lawrence). As students are arriving at school, it would always baffle my mind that students would get out of cars in front of the school building with music blasting! Now, for some kids, they would be dancing while gathering their backpacks and coats. Other kids seem to be completely oblivious of the noise level. Being in love with you has to start with being aware of what or who you are listening to. Scripture suggests that "Faith comes by hearing the word of God." In order to increase your faith, you have to absorb scripture. You have to listen until your spirit becomes one with the word. This is the same concept that must be used in learning how to love you. You have to surround yourself with people who feed your spirit while affirming who you shall be. They will feed you faith about who you are. You are the head and not the tail. You are more than a conqueror. When your heart is full of who God says you are, you will then transfer that knowledge to how you feel about you. Keep in mind people who are assigned to you will not always speak words that make you feel good. Sometimes you will need that conversation that forces you to see yourself for who you really are. You will get mad and even dislike how you feel and who pushed you there. Keep this person in your world because that is a pure form of love when someone can risk you getting mad at them in order to wake you up!

Music feeds the soul. It nourishes the heart. What music are you ingesting on a regular basis? Does it cultivate who you are? Does it remind you of your worth? Does it activate the love of God and the love you have for yourself? I can listen to the same song fifty times and hear something different each time. Last night I listened to an interview on

Facebook of a noted gospel music songwriter. He had on a sweatshirt that said, "Music is my love language." I love that! To be in love with you and to stay in love with you, create a playlist that speaks to your love language, your soul, and your future.

Now, just like Hallmark movies have main characters who drive the love story, *who are the main characters in your life?* The main characters tell a story that connects to the audience. A great actor will cause you to see yourself in some way throughout a movie. The main characters or the influential people in your life will do the same thing. They will influence how you view your life. These people can turn you toward your authentic self, or they will run you away from it. Main characters can turn a good script into an Oscar-nominated movie. They can also lead you toward a life of self-doubt and complacency or a life of endless possibilities and victorious living.

In the movies, there is always an issue. This is a problem that evolves throughout the entire movie. Many times the problem is not solved until the last thirty seconds of the movie. Once this problem is solved, you fully understand why the main character endured. Now, yes, this is a movie, but at the same time, it brings up a huge dilemma in being in love with you. *What issues have been looming in your life for all of your life?* What situations are you afraid to confront? Is it an abusive past? Is it a manipulative spouse? Is it a season of poor decisions?

I absolutely love Queen Mother Iyanla Vanzant. She has a show on the Own Network titled Fix My Life. She goes into the lives of people to "disrupt patterns" that have led to heartache and dysfunctional behaviors and relationships. She has so many one-liners from that show, but my favorite one is "Sometimes you have to call a thing a thing." In order to be in love with you, you have to confront what has shaped who you have become. My parents divorced when I was about nine years old. I remember the day my dad left. I wasn't really sad, but now I see that the experience caused me to expect men to leave me. I never had high expectations for relationships to last. As soon as I started dating, I automatically looked for reasons why they would leave or reasons for me to leave. I wanted a commitment but avoided it. I was afraid to take the risk to really love. It took time in therapy and years of a lot of inner work for me to recognize why I had settled for that idea.

Being Be You-ti-ful "in love" means accepting who you are, what you have endured, embracing the people who aided in your development, and being open to love again without fear. The movies give you a great Hollywood love story, but your life can give you the blueprint for a life of purpose, inner fulfillment, and realistic love with others and yourself.

[be you.ti.ful]

#beyoutifulprayerforbeinginlove

Help me to accept how I loved in the past,
Help me to accept how I love in my present,
Help me to accept love for my own life,
and the love of my life.

Conclusion

Here we are at the conclusion of this Be You-ti-ful journey. It is my sincere prayer that this book has started the process of investigating the areas of your life that need change. The stories, experiences, and situations I exposed to you took place over the course of several years, so please don't think that this process will evolve overnight. Here are a few elements that I want you to walk away with as a result of reading this book.

Take Your Time

Decide where you want to start digging deep into your life to find the areas that require change. Don't try to attack everything at once. One area takes time to completely unpack. Don't rush the process. Use the bonus section of this book to help you decide where you may need to start.

Get Help

I sought out professional counseling. If you get to a point where you need assistance in order to navigate through your healing, please seek out professional help. Yes, we should pray. Yes, we should believe in God; however, get help if you need it. There is no judgment in getting what you need in order to be your best self.

Accountability

During this time, try not to make major decisions in your life without wise counsel. Many times the trauma that you are processing can cloud your judgment. A mentor or accountability partner can help you break down the areas of your life that may be hard for you to see.

It has been my honor to share with you what I know God has deposited into me. Reach out to me to share how this book has impacted you or any life lessons you have learned. Let's continue to become Be You-ti-ful together.

a Wellness Start Up

I n order to Be You-ti-ful, it is important to have a consistent health and wellness routine. Here is a list of how to start your own wellness routine or jumpstart one that you have already started but you found difficult to be consistent.

Declutter—Start looking at your living spaces. This could be your home, at work, or even your car. Research shows that decluttering leads to reducing stress, aids in minimizing anxiousness, and ultimately gives you an overall peaceful spirit.

Relationship Inventory—Answer the questions below. This will help you start the process of investigating what relationships really work for you, your journey, and your destiny.

- Who helps you?
- Who motivates you?
- Who challenges you?
- Who emotionally drains you?
- Who distracts you?

Financial Fix Up—Take a good strong look at your financial health. Find a financial advisor at your local bank or credit union. Allow them to pull your credit and create a monthly budget that you will commit to. This may be difficult to do initially if this has not been your ritual, but it will have huge benefits in the long run.

Spiritual Setup—Decide what you have to do to keep your spirit full. Do you need to create time to a weekly study of scripture? Do you need to take notes during sermons at church? Do you need to find YouTube videos or a podcast? Whatever it is, find it and set yourself up to stay full.

Night Time—Create a nightly routine. I have found that once I started this, I looked forward to it. This is what I do, but you create a routine that works for you.

- End your day no later than 8 p.m. (if possible)
- Take a warm shower or bath using aromatherapy shower gels, body washes, and lotion. (Lavender is the best!)
- Find your favorite pj's or go shopping to get a cute pair!
- Have a "bed book" on your nightstand that you can read just to calm your mind and spirit. Try to stay away from anything controversial. A meditation book or even poetry will work best.
- Leave that cell phone alone!

Date Day—If you are single, decide a day that you will do something fun. Go to a movie, get a massage, go to a local café, or sit in front of a fireplace and just breathe. If you are married or have a special someone take turns planning dates. It could be as simple as having a stay-at-home movie night or dressing up and have a night at the symphony or a jazz concert…Whatever you do, stay in the moment and just have fun.

Give—Find someone to do something for. I have found that getting your mind off of yourself can help you find perspective in what's really important. As I am typing this section of the book, I plan on sending an email to just tell someone "thank you." This not only will bless the person, but it will also build you.

Cook—Now for me, during the Covid pandemic, I developed a newfound love for cooking. I realize that some people may not have that desire. Cooking a dish or a dessert from scratch gives you a sense of accomplishment. You have to plan. You have to focus. If for yourself or for someone else, take one day a week and just cook! Remember, YouTube is the best teacher!

Work It—Physical fitness is a must in order to be at your best. What I have found is the importance of finding an exercise regimen that is fun! Now treadmills and weight lifting is mandatory for some, but I love to dance. I found a hip-hop workout video on YouTube. I look forward to moving my living room furniture and just going for it! Just find what works for you and have fun doing it!

Try It—For years, I was never open to trying new things. I was in a cycle of wearing the same clothes, eating the same foods, going to the same stores, or even taking the same route to work. Sometimes to jumpstart change in your life, trying something new gives you a sense of adventure. Reading a new book, going to a new restaurant, or even watching a documentary makes you more of an interesting person. It expands your mind. Try it!

The Be You-ti-ful Circle

Group Study

If you have a Bible study group, women's ministry group, or a few friends who have a need to make more time for themselves, go to www.beyoutifulthebook.com and download instructions, videos, and a workbook. Let's become Be You-ti-ful together!

A Be You-ti-ful Cup of love

This entire process of becoming Be You-ti-ful may be over-whelming at first. There is a lot to digest. To help to soothe your spirit while doing the work, I suggest finding a warm drink or "cup of love."

You'll Need

- Get your favorite coffee mug or go shopping for one.
- 1 green tea bag
- ½ teaspoon of apple cider vinegar
- ½ teaspoon of organic honey
- 1-2 lemon slices

Directions

If you have a cute teapot, take it out and brew about 2 cups of water. If you don't have a teapot, bring 2 cups of water to a bowl using a small saucepan. Add a green tea bag to your mug and add water. Then add apple cider vinegar, organic honey, and lemon slices. Stir and enjoy!

About the Author

Lady Sylvia Marie Watkins

Radio • TV Personality • Host • Broadcaster
Writer • Producer
Speaker • Event Planner
Author • Educator
Thought Leader

God continues to elevate women in this day and time. He takes ordinary people and ordains them for a work of major proportions and magnitudes. Sylvia Marie Watkins is by no stretch of the imagination just ordinary. Virtue + Excellence = Anointing would best describe Lady Sylvia. This lady of excellence from St. Louis Missouri has made her presence felt on local scenes and continues to make waves on many national stages. Sylvia was the co-business manager of National Recording Artist Chris & Kyle w/True Spirit for fourteen years. This platform allowed Sylvia to share stages with and produced several ministry events and concerts with the likes of Donald Lawrence, Tonex, Troy Sneed, Israel Houghton & New Breed, Donnie McClurkin, Karen Clark-Sheard, Actress Jennifer Lewis, 2001 Miss America First Runner Up Monica Hardin and the list goes on and on.

In May of 2008, Sylvia completed her Master's Degree in Education Administration from Lindenwood University. Sylvia has been a public school educator for over twenty years.

When Sylvia was sixteen, she became Debutante of the Year for the National Convention of Gospel Choirs and Choruses in Baltimore, Maryland, where at the time, the Late Bishop Kenneth Moales was the president. As a result of this experience, Sylvia fell in love with the concept and process of debutante balls and event planning. Mrs. Dorothy Edgar from Teaneck, New Jersey, taught Sylvia every inch of the debutante event planning process. As a result of this training, Sylvia found her passion of coordinating and producing events and debutante balls for Christian young ladies and men. After assisting in many balls across the country, in 2006, Sylvia formally organized LadySyl Consulting Firm. LadySyl offers church ministries, conventions, as well as public and private organizations customized events. Sylvia has traveled extensively and participated in customized events for the National Convention of Gospel Choirs & Choruses, Gospel Music Workshop of America, International Church of God Sanctified, St. Louis Gospel Choral Union, Choraleers of St. Louis, St. Luke Baptist Church, Liberty Baptist Church, Prince of Peace Baptist Church and New Sunnymount Baptist Church. Sylvia has also been blessed to be a guest speaker at several ministerial conferences, high schools, and churches to motivate, encourage, and inspire people to pursue their divine destiny. Sylvia was also featured on the internationally televised show Julie and Friends on the TCT Network. In addition to her personal ministry, Sylvia was the event coordinator of the Power of Change Christian Center in Cahokia, Illinois, for fifteen years, where the pastors are Bishop Henry & Dr. Patricia Phillips. As Events Coordinator, she was able to spearhead life-changing events such as the 2014 year-long celebration of the 20th Anniversary of the pastors that culminated with a jaw-dropping, life-changing, made-for-television salute.

Sylvia's servant spirit came from her father, the late Willie Ray Watkins, who spent his life being of service to others. Her commitment to her calling through excellence was inspired by her grandmother Jennie Stevenson, her mother, Professor Anita Watkins Stevens, and her brother, music director and gospel recording artist Minister Christopher Watkins.

Recognizing the scripture Ecclesiastes 3:1, "To everything there is a time and season," Sylvia has entered into the next chapter of her life. Upon meeting business executive Laura Scarborough in a chance encounter, Sylvia was offered the opportunity to become a part of the online magazine family LLlive Magazine. Sylvia had a monthly column titled "Be You-ti-ful" which was in the "Fresh Start" segment of the magazine. "Be You-ti-ful" is all about embracing who you are called to be. It's about not allowing the titles and labels that others may have put on you or the titles you may have put on yourself to hinder you from being "true to you." It's about embracing the transitions of life and walking into the "Best Days" of your life. It's about letting go of fear and pronouncing who you shall be. Each month Sylvia unfolded topics that are prevalent to the times and seasons that we live in. Topics that Sylvia investigated were transitions, life changes, passion, purpose, health and wellness, beauty and fashion, relevant politics, the leadership and destiny of today's church, and music therapy (which included music that speaks to your core) as well as hearing from the top singers, songwriters, produces, and event planners who have captured the true meaning of their calling.

Upon meeting celebrity comedian Darius Bradford, Sylvia was asked to co-host The Darius Bradford Morning Show on Praise 99.5 FM. Sylvia gave a spiritual twist to practical life issues each morning Monday-Friday from 6 a.m.–9 a.m. Sylvia went on to have her own show on Praise 99.5fm Be You-ti-ful w/Lady Syl. This platform allowed Sylvia to spread a message of being true to who God has called you to be despite the many transitions in life. Lady Sylvia also started working on a special feature presentation/show on STL TV titled Discovering the New You, which aired on Charter Channel 198. In the summer of 2016, Lady Sylvia joined Dynasty Television and began taping her own show, Be You-ti-ful w/LadySyl, which also aired in the summer of 2016. The first airing of Be You-ti-ful was the highest viewed show in Dynasty Television history.

In the summer of 2020, Lady Syl was blessed with the opportunity to bring Lady Syl presents: "Be You-ti-ful" to the Preach the Word Network, which has a viewership of over 50 million people. Lady Syl will use this platform to continue her journey of bringing the lives of influential Atlanta citizens to the small screen. Her objective will be to give a platform to their pursuit of living an authentic life, how they values themselves, and how they knew what they had been called to do.

In the summer of 2021 Lady Syl will start working on her Doctorate Degree. In her free time, she likes cooking vegan dishes, shopping, traveling, planning events, and writing. Sylvia looks forward to adopting and embracing a Be You-ti-ful love in the future.